FRIENDS

Presented to

from

FOREVER

C0-ATW-269

A best friend
is someone
to celebrate!

I Celebrate You,™
Best Friend!

Illustrated by Beverly Burge

COUNTRYMAN

Be silly or sophisticated, wacky or cool, but always be you!

These are some
of the things I like about you:

_____

_____

_____

_____

_____

_____

_____

_____

Side by side
you and me,
sharing laughter,
swapping secrets—
this friendship was
meant to be!

You can't be anyone
else but you.
But, hey, that's
cool!

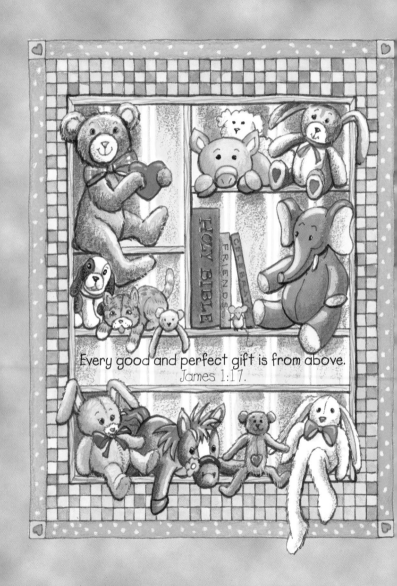

Every good and perfect gift is from above.
James 1:17.

A best friend like you makes all the
difference. This is one way you
have made a difference in my life:

_____

_____

_____

_____

_____

_____

_____

Laughing together and crying together, makes us better friends together.

You deserve a standing ovation for

_____

_____

_____

_____

_____

_____

_____

_____

To have a friend
brings happiness.
To be a friend
spreads kindness.

I love platform shoes,
They chase away the blues.
But what is really cool,
Is having a friend like you!

Some of the fun things I
enjoy doing with you are

The flavors of friendship:

Bubble Gum—
a best friend sticks around,
through thick and thin.

Grape Jelly—
a best friend helps out
when you're in a jam.

Mint Chip—
a best friend is cool and sweet.

Red Hot Cinnamon—
a best friend spices up dull days.

A Friend Is...

F _____

R _____

I _____

E _____

N _____

D _____

FOREVER

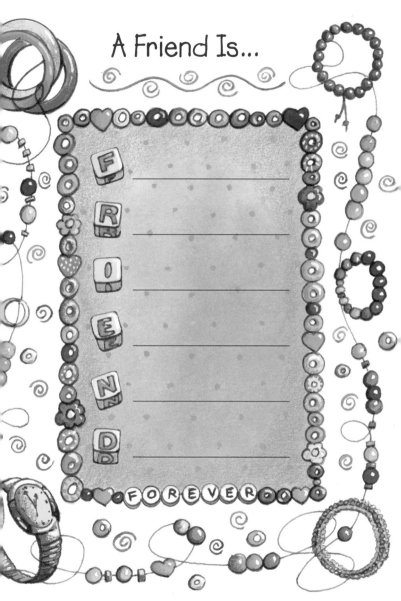

A life
without
friends is
like a year
without
summer.

FRIENDS

A best friend says, "You go, girl!"
Here is my dream for you:

_____

_____

_____

_____

_____

_____

Thank you God

for this best friend

that you gave to me.

For without a friend like her,

how boring life would be!

I celebrate you!

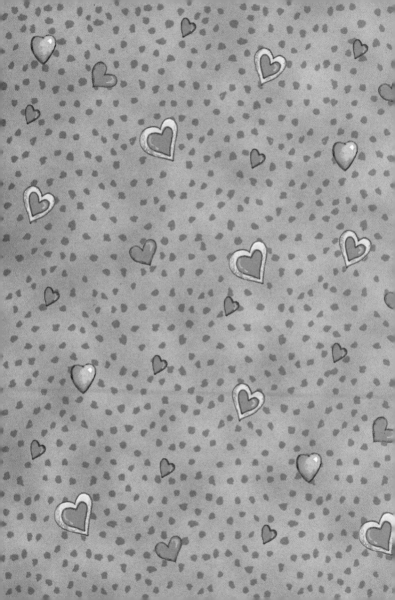